# making a difference
## the save the world handbook

Ali Cronin

ticktock

First published in Great Britain in 2009 by ticktock Media Ltd,
The Old Sawmill, 103 Goods Station Road, Tunbridge Wells, Kent, TN1 2DP

*ticktock project editor: Victoria Garrard*
*ticktock project designer: Sara Greasley*
*With thanks to Martin Cullen and Friends of the Earth*

ISBN-13: 978-1-84696-955-3 pbk
Printed in China
9 8 7 6 5 4 3 2 1

Picture credits (t=top; b=bottom; c=centre; l=left; r=right):
age fotostock/SuperStock: 16. Bettmann/Corbis: 5t. Image Source/SuperStock: 1.
iStock: 23t. Jason Alden/Rex Features: 38. Jupiter Images: 36.
Sara Greasley and Hayley Terry: OFCb, 6t, 10t, 12b, 15t, 20, 22, 26 both, 28br, 31b, 33b, 34t, 39, 40l, OBCcl, OBCcr. Shutterstock: 2, 4, 8t, 8-9, 9t, 10b, 11, 13 all, 14, 15b, 17t, 18, 19, 21, 23b, 24, 27, 28l, 29, 32t, 32b, 30, 31t, 33t, 34bl, 35, 37, 40r, 41 all, 42, 43, 47.
ticktock Media Archive: OFCt, OBCt.

# contents

# introduction

Our planet is in trouble. If we don't do something about it now, we will face storms and floods, the possibility of losing coastal towns to the sea and the extinction of some plants and animals. The air in our towns and cities is already dangerously polluted.

# Make a difference!

One person really can make a difference. Look at...
- Florence Nightingale
- Martin Luther King
- Marie Curie
- Gandhi

...all ordinary people who achieved amazing things.
Why shouldn't you be one of them?

# Who said that?

"You must be the change you wish to see in the world."

(In other words, don't expect anything to happen if you wait for someone else to do it...)

*Gandhi, leader of Indian independence movement and peaceful protest pioneer.*

## How to be the change

- This book contains hundreds of ideas for ways you can look after the planet. From the three Rs of Reduce, Reuse, Recyle to peaceful protest, from food to fashion, from staying in to, er, going out.
- You could be changing the world 24 hours a day – even while you sleep – and this book shows you how (it's generous like that).
- Read it and weep. Then get angry. Then do something about it. Yee-ha!

## A disclaimer

Doing your bit for the environment has to fit in with your life. There are things mentioned in this book that everyone can do, like turning off the lights when you leave a room. But some things depend on factors like location and money. Doing your bit means doing what you can – without changing who you are. Now go get 'em, tiger.

# quiz: are you naturally green?

**You know the theory, but how do you live your life? Do the quiz and find out if living the eco way comes naturally to you...**

**1) What's your morning routine?**
**a)** Get the shower running, use the loo while the water's heating up, then hop in for a quick freshen up and a hair wash
**b)** Use the loo, brush teeth, then jump in the shower to wash my hair
**c)** Use the loo, brush teeth, then on alternate days have a quick wash from the sink or a shower to wash my hair

**2) How do you dry your hair?**
**a)** Blow dryer and straighteners
**b)** Blow dryer
**c)** I usually let it dry naturally

**3) What do you have for breakfast?**
**a)** My choice from a selection pack of cereals
**b)** Nothing – I'll pick something up later
**c)** Either toast or cereal from a big box

**4) How do you get to school?**
**a)** My mum gives me a lift on her way to work

**b)** I catch the bus

**c)** I walk or cycle

### 5) What do you have for lunch?

**a)** A hot meal from the school canteen

**b)** A sandwich from the school canteen

**c)** Sandwiches I've brought from home

### 6) What do you drink throughout the day?

**a)** A few cans of fizz or small cartons of juice

**b)** Water from the cooler

**c)** I bring a sports bottle of water from home

### 7) What's your bedtime routine?

**a)** Watch TV or listen to music till I drop off

**b)** Watch TV in bed for a while, then lights off

**c)** Read for a bit, then lights off

## Answers

**Mostly a's: Faintly Green**

You know how to be green, but you haven't yet let it into your life. Your answers indicate that you're wasting either water, energy, packaging or all three. But being green doesn't have to mean changing your whole existence. If your hair looks rubbish without straighteners, consider turning your weekly soak in the bath into a fortnightly one to redress the balance. It's all about compromise.

**Mostly b's: Green**

You are taking definite steps to be green, but there are some areas where you haven't compromised. Almost everyone who cares about the planet is the same: we're only human, after all. Just make sure that your reasons are sound. Getting the bus to school because it would be a three-mile walk is fine. Leaving your TV on standby overnight because you can't be bothered to get out of bed to turn it off is less so!

**Mostly c's: Saintly Green**

You are greener than the contents of Shrek's hanky. Whether it's coincidence or a definite decision, your life is all about the eco. You choose the energy-efficient, low-packaging options, which in general are not only good for the planet, but cheaper too. Can't say fairer than that.

# carbon footprint

## What is a 'carbon footprint' and how does it work?

### Clue: it doesn't involve actual feet!

- Your carbon footprint is the amount of $CO_2$ (carbon dioxide) you release through burning fossil fuels every day (when people say something uses a lot of energy, they mean it releases a lot of $CO_2$).

- Watching TV, using the internet, travelling by car ... these all use fossil fuels.

- And too much $CO_2$ is A Bad Thing because it contributes to the greenhouse effect* and global warming.

- The larger our carbon footprint, the more damage we're doing to the environment.

## What does carbon neutral mean?

- The ideal is to become carbon neutral, which we can do by calculating our carbon footprint and then offsetting it by, for example, growing our own fruit and veg and recycling.
- Offsetting is like going for a run after eating too much: it cancels out the damage you've done.

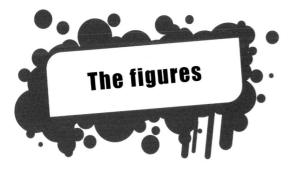

**The figures**

- You can calculate your footprint at zerofootprintkids.com/kids_home.aspx.
- Offsetmycarbonfootprint.com has info on how to – doh! – offset your carbon footprint (click on 'CO2 Reduction'), although it's aimed at adults so it may be something to print out and leave lying around at home, casually like.

* Fear not, jargon-phobes: all eco words and phrases are explained in the glossary on page 44.

# recycling

## Once is definitely not enough. Remember to recycle!

- Think of the stuff you throw away: a drink can on the way to school, a plastic bottle at lunchtime, the paper you get through during the day. All of it could be recycled.
- Recycling uses way less energy and resources than making stuff from scratch, and cuts down on all that plastic, glass and metal hanging around in landfill for centuries.
- In short, recycling is vital if you want to save the planet.

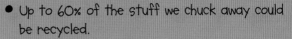
## Scary facts-arama

- Up to 60% of the stuff we chuck away could be recycled.
- The UK produces over 450,000 tons of plastic bottles every year – of which a piffling 5% are recycled.
- 70% less energy is needed to recycle paper than to make it from scratch.
- One recycled can saves enough energy to power a TV for three hours.
- It takes up to 500 years for plastic to decompose.
- Landfill sites (where our rubbish is dumped) can produce gases that contribute to acid rain and global warming.

# How, where and what to recycle

**1)** Just a few of the gazillion (OK, not the official figure) things we can recycle: CDs, exercise books, junk mail, magazines, glass bottles, food and drink cans, carrier bags, yoghurt pots, bikes, clothes, batteries, computers, mobile phones, TVs, musical instruments and toys.

**2)** In the UK enter your postcode at recyclenow.com to see what you can recycle, or to request a free recycling box.

**3)** Get into the habit of separating waste paper, food packaging, different coloured glass bottles, etc, so you can easily put them out for recycling.

**4)** Do a web search for 'recycling boxes' to find sites that sell them.

## Did You Know?

That fleece your nan wears could well be made out of recycled plastic bottles. Which goes some way to making up for its total lack of style.

# the really good rubbish quiz

**You chuck something in the bin, it ends up in landfill... But how long before it breaks down to nothing? Do the quiz and find out...**

**1) Glass bottle**
a) 100 years
b) 1000 years
c) 1000000 years

**2) Plastic bag**
a) 1 year
b) 20 years
c) 200 years

**3) Plastic bottle**
a) 50 years
b) 500 years
c) 5000 years

**4) Aluminium can**
a) 20 years
b) 100 years
c) 500 years

**5) Newspaper**
a) A week
b) A month
c) A year

**6) Apple core**
a) Two days
b) Two weeks
c) Two months

**7) Banana skin**
a) Two weeks
b) Two months
c) Two years

# Answers

**1) Glass bottle: c)** Glass takes forever to break down. Literally. A bottle thrown into landfill yesterday will still be there in a million years. But the good news is that glass is also endlessly recyclable.

**2) Plastic bag: b)** The average British household uses 364 plastic bags every year. That's a massive amount of potential rubbish – unless, of course, we recycle 'em.

**3) Plastic bottle: b)** Although actually that's an estimate, as no one really knows how long plastic takes to break down because it hasn't been around for long enough. For all we know it could take thousands of years.

**4) Aluminium can: c)** Aluminium is another one that's built to last, not least because it doesn't rust. Think of all the drink cans you've ever chucked away: they're still in landfill.

**5) Newspaper: b)** Newspaper breaks down pretty easily, although some researchers have found newspapers in landfill that were over 15 years old. And there's really no excuse for not recycling paper.

**6) Apple core: c)** But put it on a compost heap and it will biodegrade down into garden food. Find out more on page 47.

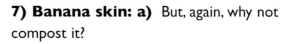

**7) Banana skin: a)** But, again, why not compost it?

# saving energy and water

**One of the fundamentals of living your life the eco way is saving energy. And the good news is that you can do it at the flick of a switch.**

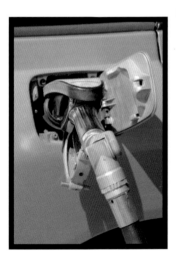

## Scary stats

Like Sci-Fi, only true!

- Estimates vary, but it is thought that within the next 50 years – and probably sooner – there will no longer be enough of the fossil fuels oil (petrol) and gas to go around.
- There is enough coal – another fossil fuel – to last at least 150 years. But if we keep using coal, global warming will keep getting worse.
- Americans make up 5% of the world's population, but use 24% of the world's energy.

## Save the planet while you sleep

Before you turn in, turn off your TV, DVD player, PC and games consoles at the wall. Over 10% of household electricity is wasted on appliances on standby. Turn off the lights and you'll save 60 watts of energy per bulb per hour (that's a lot of energy, maths fans). Sleep well!

# Will our water run out?

You'd think that water was the ultimate renewable resource, since the planet is covered with the stuff. Not true. What you are about to read may freak you out. Look at the facts…

- Just 3% of the world's water is fresh (as opposed to salt), and most of that is frozen. Just 1% is suitable for human use.
- Without fresh water we could not exist.
- The world's population will probably increase by about 45% in the next 30 years. The amount of available fresh water is likely to increase by just 10%.
- UNESCO predicts that by 2020 water shortage will be a serious worldwide problem.

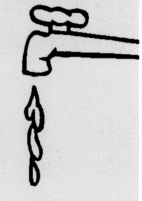

## What can we do?

## Five steps to using and wasting less

**1)** Turn off the tap while you brush your teeth and save up to five litres of water a minute.

**2)** A three-minute shower uses up to a third less water than a bath.

**3)** Phone your home's water company and ask for a free displacement device to put in your toilet cistern. It'll save water (and the bill payer's money) with every flush.

**4)** If you have a dishwasher, only turn it on when it's full. If you don't have a dishwasher, do the washing up in a full bowl rather than washing everything under the tap.

**5)** Keep a jug of water in the fridge rather than running the tap until it runs cold every time you have a drink.

# The easiest way EVER to save water

Wee in the shower! It saves a flush. Or, if you think that's too disgusting, consider only flushing the toilet when you, ahem, really need to.

# transport: getting there

## Most of us get in a car or on a bus or train nearly every day. But what's the environmental impact?

## The ex(haust) files

We all know that cars, planes and buses are bad for the environment but which has the worst emissions (measured in g of $CO_2$ per km)?

### 1) Plane
Air travel is likely to be the biggest part of your carbon footprint and is top in the terrible transport league. Emissions of 210–460g/km per person are similar to a large car but we tend to travel hundreds of kilometres by plane so the total emissions are very high.

### 2) Large Car
If you are driven to and from school in a gas–guzzler, you are creating one heck of a carbon footprint for yourself.

Large cars have approximate emissions of 200–500g/km.

### 3) Car
An average–sized car emits 160–200g of $CO_2$ per km.

### 4) Train
Rail travel emissions work out at 40–165g/km.

### 5) Bus
The bus is best (104g/km) because of the amount of people who can fit on.

# What about cycling?

- If you have a bike, it's a great eco-friendly option.
- If you don't have a bike and reckon you'd ride it every day, consider getting one.
- Even better, because making a new bike from scratch uses a lot of energy, get a second-hand one, and shrink your carbon footprint even more.

## Walk ... and live longer!

Walking places takes longer, but you'll have an attractive glow about you when you finally get there!

- Brisk walking improves stamina, energy and even life expectancy.
- It is good exercise and excellent for toning your abs (stomach muscles), bum and legs. It can even define your arm muscles, if you swing them jauntily enough.
- Brisk walking can burn up to 400 calories per hour.

## You can do it!

"If you think you can do a thing or think you can't do a thing, you're right."

*Henry Ford (1863-1947),
founder of the Ford Motor Company which
revolutionised American industry. Not at all
eco-friendly, but apparently he was a nice man.*

# volunteering

## It's the perfect way to do more towards saving our planet and it looks good on your CV: nice!

### Volunteer vitals

- Decide how much time you can spare for volunteering.
- Then, search for volunteering opportunities at do-it.org.uk.
- It will be harder to find official opportunities if you're under 16, so you might need to be creative. Asking if a nearby school or old people's home needs help with gardening, for example. Or offering your services to a charity shop.

## Real-life story

" I started out volunteering at my local common ... now I'm about to spend three weeks in Peru!

I didn't want to volunteer at all. I was looking forward to spending the summer lying in the garden and watching TV, but my best friend persuaded me to join her in a team clearing weeds at our local common.

It turned out to be the best two weeks of my life! I made new friends – and new muscles – all while getting a tan!

I had caught the volunteering bug, so straight away I started applying for volunteering posts abroad. I focused on conservation and looking after our planet, as that's what I feel most strongly about.

I got the letter a week ago. I've been accepted on a wildlife conservation expedition in the Amazon! It'll be backbreaking work, there'll be poisonous bugs, and I'll be sleeping on the ground. I can't wait! "

Sam, 17

## Did you know?

Volunteering was voted the second greatest source of individual joy in a survey. What came first? Dancing!

## You can do it!

"You must do the thing you think you cannot do."

*Eleanor Roosevelt (1884-1962), an advocate for civil rights, author and speaker. She was married to American President Franklin D. Roosevelt.*

# it's for charity

## I want to do more, how can I help a charity?

Another way you can help the environment is by raising money for charity. Sponsored events are a good place to start. Here's how to do it…

### Five steps to doing it for cash

**1)** Choose your charity. The further information section on page 46 has links.

**2)** Choose an event for which you can be sponsored. It could be anything from reading books to running a marathon. Anything goes, as long as it's safe and people are prepared to give you money for it.

**3)** Organise sponsorship. The easiest way of doing this is via an online donations site, like justgiving.com. (Your friends will need access to a credit or debit card to donate in this way.)

**4)** Do your thing. If it's not a public event, have an adult there to watch and confirm that you did what you set out to do.

**5)** Watch the money mount up. Sweet!

## Real-life story

" I raised over £500 for charity just by doing what I love.

I've been into skating since I was 11. I skate everywhere and spend most weekends at the skatepark.

The charity thing started when I saw the movie 'An Inconvenient Truth' on TV. It's a documentary about **global warming**. I only watched it 'cause nothing else was on, but it was amazing.

My friends weren't impressed when I said I was going to do sponsored kickflips (a skating move), but I didn't care what they thought. To be honest, the movie had scared me, and I wanted to do something to help.

I got everyone I knew to sponsor me and emailed the local paper who ran a story on it. In the end I raised £574 for environmental charities. It felt good."

Matt, 16

# Easy ways to raise money

Don't have time? Here's how to raise money for charity without breaking a sweat.

### 1) Texting

Get your friends and family to give you money for every half-day you can go without sending a text. Yep, it's a toughie.

### 2) Walking

A sponsored no-transport day. Ask people to sponsor you for every mile you walk during a normal day. All you need is a pedometer (from about £7) and you're set.

### 3) Gaming

Finally, all those hours getting repetitive strain injury in your thumbs pays off. Do a sponsored game-athon and get your friends to pay up for every level you complete.

### 4) TV

A sponsored no-watch. Ask people to sponsor you for every day you can go without turning on the telly / watching stuff online.

### 5) Junk Food

Get your friends to cough up for every day you can go without junk food. That means no cans of Coke, no chocolate, no crisps. You'll be healthy AND raising money for charity. Win-win or what?

# making your voice heard

## Do you want to change the world? Then tell the world!

You don't have to tie yourself to the gates of Parliament and bellow slogans to make your voice heard (you'd be arrested, for a start). Here are five simple things you can do.

**1)** Find your MP at writetothem.com and write to them. Ask them if they plan to ensure your town or city becomes carbon neutral, and if not, why not. Tell them why you believe becoming carbon neutral is important.

**2)** Write an email to your local newspaper's letters page explaining why we need to do something about saving our planet. Urge everyone reading your email to reuse and recycle. You could even mention this book. And include your age – they're more likely to print your views if they know you're not an adult. Weird, but true.

**3)** Why not send your email to the national press too? But don't send a group email. No newspaper will print your letter if they know you've also sent it to their rivals.

**4)** Consider forming an environmental group at school, or joining an existing one. There's strength in numbers, and together you can start petitions, put on presentations and raise awareness.

**5)** Join a local action group. Do a web search for 'Environmental action groups [put name of your town here]' to find any near you.

## Does Protesting Work?

Of course! If it hadn't been for peaceful protest, the following may never have happened...

- Women getting the vote.
- The 999 emergency phone number.
- Fashion chains changing the way their clothes are sourced.
- Three years of protesting led to the UK Climate Change Bill.
- And through Gandhi — the father of peaceful protest himself — India's independence from British rule in 1947.

### You can do it!

"You haven't failed till you stop trying."

*Anon*

# the future's green

## Thinking about making a career out of saving the planet? Read on for some of your options.

## At School

### What to study

The sciences, geography, geology, engineering, business, marketing, media and communications are all useful subjects to study if you eventually want a job doing eco stuff.

## Your Future

The careers that could be waiting for you...

### Conservationist

- From rainforest research in the Ecuadorian Amazon to coordinating a local wildlife centre, conservationists work towards protecting natural resources and securing their future. You could help animals, birds, the sea, rivers, forests, deserts or even the air we breathe.
- Find out more at naturenet.net/people/careers.html

## Teacher

- Whether you run educational programmes at conservation centres, teach geography to school students or become an academic and teach environmental science at a university, there are many ways you can pass on your knowledge and passion for protecting the environment.
- Find out more at tda.gov.uk/recruit/becomingateacher.aspx

## Campaigner

- A job in campaigning means working towards spreading awareness and persuading others to take your point of view all day, five days a week.
- This could be in the marketing or communications department of an environmental organisation, or perhaps fundraising for a charity.
- Go to environmentjob.co.uk to browse some current campaigning posts.

## Journalist

- Lots of journalists have specialisms. You could work towards writing about environmental issues for newspapers and magazines, or getting a job on an eco magazine.
- Go to prospects.ac.uk/links/pubjournal for tips on getting into journalism.

## Retail

- A Saturday job in a charity shop could give you the skills to start working towards opening your own ethical fashion store.
- Before you know it, you could have the eco version of Topshop or Banana Republic on your hands.
- Go to targetjobs.co.uk/retail/default.aspx to find out about following a career in retail.

# home-grown talent

## I want to grow my own food but don't know where to start...

Growing your own food and composting your food waste is a brilliant way of offsetting your carbon footprint by cutting down on food miles (the distance food has to travel from the place where it's grown to your local supermarket). Home-grown food also tastes better and costs less. What's not to love?

## Dear Daisy

**Gardening agony aunt Daisy Chain (totally her real name) solves your home-growing problems.**

**Q.** I don't have a garden, so how can I grow my own food?

**A.** Easily. Tomatoes, potatoes, spinach and strawberries are just four of the veg and herbs you can grow in pots. bbcgreen.com/food/grow-your-own/container-gardening has detailed info.

**Q.** I like the idea of growing my own, but I know that I'll forget to look after them.

**A.** Nah. You could do it in ad breaks if you wanted. Just water your plants every couple of days (every day in the summer) and weed them every couple of weeks. 10 minutes each time. Done.

**Q.** I don't own a gross old jumper with soil-encrusted cuffs. Can I still be a gardener?

**A.** A gross old jumper is only required if you're male and over 50. Phew, eh?

## Mmm, tasty!

Composting garden and kitchen waste returns essential nutrients to the food chain and makes plants big and strong.

### Ingredients

A compost bin (get one online for around £5)

Banana skins, apple cores, veg peelings, used tea bags, egg shells, egg boxes, the odd worm.

### Not ingredients

Cooked food, meat, dairy products, dog and cat poo (like you'd considered it!).

### Method

Chuck all ingredients into compost bin. Leave for six to nine months but remember to give it an occasional shake up. When it's ready the stuff at the bottom will be rich, dark brown, crumbly and sweet smelling. Spread on your garden. Feel smug.

# ethical food shopping

**Biting off more than you can chew? Take steps to ensure your dinner doesn't cost the Earth.**

## Five steps to reusing a carrier bag with style

1) Go to favourite, stupidly expensive store
2) Buy something small (hey, it's for the environment!)
3) Ask for a large bag
4) Fold bag and keep with you
5) Use every time you go shopping. Not a manky supermarket carrier in sight!

## Did You Know?

Around a third of all the food we buy ends up in the bin – and most of this could have been eaten.

# The perils of a tuna sandwich

Check the issues surrounding a humble sandwich. Who knew lunch could be so scary?

## BREAD

- Pre-packed bread is usually sold in plastic wrapping, which uses oil in its production and takes hundreds of years to biodegrade.
- Non-organic bread may contain traces of pesticides and usually contains artificial preservatives.

**What you can do:** Choose organic bread from the fresh bread counter. Recycle any plastic bread wrappers. Or go bonkers and bake your own.

## BUTTER

- Breeding livestock for meat and dairy products accounts for 18% of global greenhouse gas emissions.
- Animals fed a non-organic diet store toxins in their fat cells, which can find their way into milk and butter.

**What you can do:** Go for organic butter from free-range cows, or leave it out completely.

## TUNA

- Tuna is endangered and contains traces of mercury, PCBs (cancer-causing toxins) and pesticides.
- Tuna fishing often kills dolphins too.

**What you can do:** Choose 'dolphin-friendly' or 'skipjack' tuna or try tinned salmon.

## SALAD

- Bagged salad leaves are often rinsed in a chlorine solution to kill bacteria and then packaged in a modified atmosphere: oxygen is removed to make the salad last longer.
- Both these practices reduce the number of nutrients in the salad.
- Non-organic cucumbers, tomatoes, etc, often contain pesticide residues.
- There could also be food miles issues.

**What you can do:** Choose organic salad that hasn't been pre-packed. Look for seasonal produce grown as locally to you as possible to cut down on food miles or, even better, try growing your own.

# choc horror!

## How can something so darn delicious be so bad for the planet? Read it and weep...

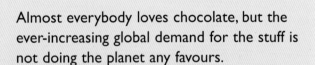

### The scary stuff

Almost everybody loves chocolate, but the ever-increasing global demand for the stuff is not doing the planet any favours.

- In the UK alone, 500 million kg of chocolate is eaten every year.
- Greater demand means that farmers have to find new ways to grow the cocoa bean crop (from which chocolate is made), resulting in massive use of harmful fertilisers and pesticides.
- Areas of rain forest are being destroyed to make way for cocoa farms, leaving animals, insects and birds homeless and causing soil erosion and water pollution.
- Farmers often get a ridiculously low price for their cocoa beans — in fact hardly any of them could afford to buy the chocolate that their cocoa beans become. This means that many of them are forced to clear even more land to sell timber or graze cattle.

## Bitter sweets

Turns out sugar isn't just bad for your teeth:

- The production of sugar crops destroys habitats to make way for plantations, uses huge amounts of water and agricultural chemicals, and spews out tons of polluted wastewater.

- And, as 145 million tons of sugars are produced in 121 countries every year, that's a lot of damage to a lot of places.

- On top of this, refining sugar to clean and whiten it uses a lot of energy. Nothing sweet about that.

## What you can do

- Look for Fair trade organic or rainforest-friendly sugar and chocolate.

- You could ask your parents if they'll buy unrefined sugar.

- Choose dark chocolate – not only is there evidence that eating it reduces the risk of heart disease and diabetes, it's also better for the environment as it doesn't contain dairy products.

- There are links in further information on page 46.

# fast food

## Fast food is full of fat, preservatives, sugar, blah blah. So far, so obvious. But what about its effect on the environment?

## Chemicals and waste – mmm, tasty!

- Fast food means lots of packaging. Cardboard burger and pizza boxes, plastic drinks lids, plastic straws and paper napkins equals a lot of potential waste.

- Polystyrene (what that foamy stuff in fast food packaging is made of) is a big polluter. It contains harmful chemicals and creates more potential waste.

- Paper napkins are only white because they've been bleached, which uses yet more nasty chemicals.

- Certain fast food places insist on their fries all being the same size. One of the ways in which they can ensure this is by creating irrigated potato farms. Clearing the land to create these farms destroys animal and plant life, and irrigation uses huge amounts of water. Not good.

## Did you know?

Producing a fast food meal of a burger, fries and a soft drink uses 6,800 litres of water. This includes the water needed to grow the potatoes, the grain for the bun and to feed the cows, and the production of the drink.

## DIY fast food

Can't do without your fast food fix? Try this incredibly easy salsa.

**1)** Heat a teaspoon of olive oil in a pan.

**2)** Add three thickly chopped garlic cloves and cook gently until golden brown.

**3)** Put the fried garlic in a bowl and add two finely chopped tomatoes, half a finely chopped red onion and a tablespoon olive oil.

**4)** Mix it all up and season with salt and pepper and some chopped flat leaf parsley.

**5)** Serve with tortilla chips.

**6)** Yum!

## Did you know?

A car that runs on diesel will usually run perfectly well on cooking oil — and emit exhaust fumes that smell like frying food. Much nicer all round. (Shame it's illegal in the UK.)

# animal products

## Does meat murder the planet? Whatever your views on killing animals for food, there are also environmental reasons for cutting down on animal products.

**Carbon hoofprint**

Animal farming causes more greenhouse gas emissions than all of the world's cars, lorries and planes put together. Here's why.

- Large amounts of animal feed are needed to produce relatively small amounts of meat or milk.
- Nitrogen fertilisers are used to produce animal feed, which uses lots of energy and emits, among others, the greenhouse gas nitrous oxide.
- Forests naturally absorb carbon dioxide, but many forests are destroyed so animals can graze or animal feed can be grown.
- The production of animal products involves a lot of food miles, usually in energy-tastic refrigerated lorries.

## Did You Know?

Cows and sheep emit greenhouse gases! Their flatulance releases methane into the atmosphere. And methane is 23 times as globally warming as $CO_2$. Gives a whole new meaning to silent but deadly.

## There's no way I could give up meat...

- Why not consider cutting down on cheap, intensively farmed or fast food meat?

- The best meat is usually organic and locally produced (it tastes nicer and is better for you too).

- You could also suggest to your parents that they find out about their meat suppliers' environmental and animal welfare standards.

# eco fashion

**Ethical shopping isn't all vegan dungarees and ugly shoes. Just a few changes could ensure you keep stylish – and a clear conscience.**

## How cruel is your T-shirt?

- More than 8,000 chemicals are used to make clothes from scratch. Many of these pollute soil and water and kill fish and other sea life.
- Making clothes also uses masses of energy and creates thousands of clothes miles.
- It's likely that some of your clothes were made by people (including children) who earn a pittance and work 10 to 12 hour days, seven days a week.
- On top of this, cheaper fashion means that we're buying more and more clothes, which creates more and more waste.

### Did you know?

Growing cotton is responsible for a scary 25% of all pesticides used. Who knew T-shirts could be so bad for the environment?

# So what can you do?

- Email the head office of your favourite fashion stores. Ask them what steps they are taking to reduce the use of chemicals in the manufacture of their clothes, how much the people who make their clothes are paid and what their working conditions are like.
- If you don't get a reply or aren't happy with their response, consider boycotting their stores. Email to tell them that this is what you are doing.
- Look for fashion brands that sell clothes made from organic (grown without using harmful pesticides) or Fair trade cotton.
- And of course the most ethical way of buying new clothes is to go vintage. Find out more – and about how to look out for celeb cast offs over the page.

## Skanky into swanky

To make old clothes look new, customising is key, people. You can cover stains, change the shape of a top, add embellishments. Here's how:

- Tops: Cut a slash neck. Cut off the sleeves and either hem or leave rough. Sew on patches or add badges/pins. Write your own slogan with fabric pens.
- Jeans: Cut off to make shorts. Sew patches onto the back pockets. Dye them a darker colour using permanent fabric dyes. Add chains.
- Jackets: Remove the sleeves. Add small button badges to the lapels. Add chains. Write a slogan on the back.
- Skirts and dresses: Make them shorter. Cut a slit in the back or sides. Sew on patches. Remove the pockets. Add new pockets. Add a new or different belt. Turn a dress into a top by cutting it off and hemming.
- Hats: Add badges or brooches.
- Look in department stores and haberdashers for fabric dye, buttons, patches, poppers and Velcro. Online auction sites like eBay™ are good for vintage or unusual pieces.

# the celeb trend that saves the world (kind of!)

Vintage fashion is the perfect trend. Celebs like the Olsen twins, Rachel Bilson and Zac Efron are all fans of vintage.

It's also cheap, eco-friendly and you'll never turn up at a party wearing the same outfit as someone else. Here's how to do it.

## Charity shop chic

- You don't need to find an expensive specialist vintage store (although do a web search if you want to find one near you).
- Nope, the best way to find vintage bargains is to look to the humble charity shop or thrift store. After all, what is vintage but a fancy word for second-hand?
- charityshops.org.uk has a list of UK charity shops, and thethriftshopper.com lists US thrift stores.

# Charity shop tips

- Mess is good. If you find a shop with freshly laundered clothes organised according to type and colour, you may be out of luck. The ultra-organised charity shop manager will usually flog off the good stuff via sites like eBay™, as this brings in more money for their charity.

- Instead you're looking for disorganised, crammed shelves and rails. This is where you're most likely to find a true vintage gem hiding among the misshapen T-shirts and vom-coloured slacks.

- Be ruthless: look through the whole shop.

- Avoid stains on an otherwise clean garment – they're unlikely to come out.

- Rummage! Get really stuck in. Look through every pile and rifle through every rail, no matter how unpromising it looks.

- Try not to look at the labels first. If it's a really embarrassing brand, you can always cut the label out. The trick is to look for good quality stuff that has kept its shape.

- Why not bring in a bag of your own cast-offs too? That way you'll doubly do your bit for the environment.

# Find celeb cast-offs!

Colleen McCloughlin takes her old clothes to the Barnado's shop in Alderley Edge, Cheshire, where she lives. Who says other celebs don't do the same? Here are some hotspots where you just might find the odd celeb cast-off. No guarantees, but isn't it worth a try?!

- North London is crawling with celebular types. Sienna Miller, Lily Allen, Kate Moss, Russell Brand, Amy Winehouse, Peaches Geldof and, er, Chris Moyles have all lived there.

- West London has been home to Estelle, Daniel Radcliffe, Sophie Ellis Bextor and Miquita Oliver.

- East London is the home base of Dizzee Rascal.

- Oxford could have some of Emma Watson's cast-offs in its charity shops.

- Surrey has been home to Fearne Cotton and Cheryl and Ashley Cole.

- Liverpool plays host to most of the Hollyoaks cast.

# the hidden cost of looking good

## Cosmetics and toiletries are often full of environmental nasties. Even toothpaste. Here are the facts.

### AFTERSHAVE & PERFUME

Perfume contains 70-85% alcohol, and is full of petro-based synthetic chemicals, both made from crude oil (a fossil fuel). Not good for your health or the environment.

**What you can do:** Choose aftershave with natural ingredients, like witch hazel, and go for natural perfumes made from essential oils.

## DEODORANT

Deodorants and antiperspirants contain petrochemicals, which release harmful chemicals into the air and water. These include formaldehyde (one of the world's most hazardous compounds) and aluminium, which is a big pollutant.

**What you can do:** Go for natural or crystal deodorants. They cost more, but last for ages.

## MAKE-UP

Make-up is chock full of hazardous chemicals, including plasticisers and formaldehyde. These are flushed down the sink when we wash off our make-up: bad news for soil, water and wildlife.

**What you can do:** Choose organic. Look for less, and recyclable, packaging.

## SANITARY PROTECTION

(Sorry lads, this is the periods bit.)
Used tampons and towels create masses of waste, a lot of which ends up in the sea, littering beaches and harming wildlife. Tampons are made from cotton, which is grown using masses of pesticides, while pads use plastics, which is polluting and energy-heavy.

**What you can do:** Look for organic towels and tampons. Wrap used products and put them in the bin, rather than flushing them down the loo.

## TOOTHPASTE

Many toothpastes contain environmental nasties like triclosan and potassium nitrate. Every time we spit, we send these chemicals down the drain and into the water system. Plastic toothpaste tubes take a lot of energy to produce and cause waste.

**What you can do:** Choose a natural toothpaste. Buy a bigger tube to cut down on packaging. Recycle the packaging. And, remember, turn off the tap while you're brushing.

# green party

## Caring about the planet doesn't mean you have to give up your social life. Get out there and party. But in a responsible, eco-friendly way, obviously.

**Eco Night Out**

**How to paint the town without tainting the planet.**

### GETTING READY

- Have a shower instead of a bath to save water.
- Turn hair straighteners off as soon as possible so you don't waste energy.
- If you want to wear something new, why not borrow from a friend or go vintage? Every time you buy something new, you increase your carbon footprint.

### GETTING THERE

- Your first priority is to stay safe. If you're going out at night either walk with friends or, if that's not an option, try to share lifts so each car is full.
- If you buy snacks at any point, think about the packaging used and remember to recycle.

### BEING THERE

If you're at a friend's house, remember to turn the light off after you use the bathroom.

Eco Night In with Friends

**How to stay eco without making a big deal of it.**

## SNACKS

- Rather than buying bagged popcorn, you can cut down on packaging by getting unpopped kernels and making your own. It's cheaper too. Add butter, sugar or salt for flavouring.
- Buy the biggest bottle of fizz you can find, rather than individual bottles or cans, to avoid yet more pesky packaging. Remember to recycle the bottle.
- Look for unbleached, recycled paper napkins or, even better, use cloth napkins.
- If you're in the mood for ice-cream or chocolate, consider buying organic or Fair trade varieties.

## ENTERTAINMENT

- Don't forget to turn your DVD player, stereo, games console and computer off at the wall when you're not using them.
- Bear in mind that the higher the volume, the more energy it's using.

## SLEEPOVERS

Try to turn off the light at some point during the night – even if it's only for a couple of hours.

# glossary

**acid rain** Rain that falls as weak acid after reacting with pollution from cars, factories and power stations.

**carbon dioxide** A gas, also known as $CO_2$, which occurs naturally and is vital for plants to grow and humans to live. The burning of fossil fuels to make energy releases carbon dioxide and contributes to the greenhouse effect and global warming.

**carbon footprint** According to carbonfootprint.com this is, "A measure of the impact our activities have on the environment, and in particular climate change. It relates to the amount of greenhouse gases produced in our day-to-day lives through burning fossil fuels for electricity, heating and transportation, etc. The carbon footprint is a measurement of all greenhouse gases we individually produce and [their] carbon dioxide equivalent."

**carbon neutral** When an individual or business has reduced or offset their $CO_2$ emissions to such an extent that they've cancelled out their carbon footprint.

**climate change** Change in long-term weather patterns (namely average temperatures and the average annual amount of rain or snow) brought about by global warming.

**clothes miles** The distance items of clothing have to travel from the place where they were made to the fashion stores that sell them. The greater the number of clothes miles, the more energy is used and the greater the carbon footprint.

**$CO_2$** The chemical formula for carbon dioxide. Say 'See Oh 2' not 'Ko 2' (in case you haven't covered it in Chemistry yet).

**compost** A mixture of decaying organic stuff (veg peelings, leaves, used tea bags, etc.) that breaks down over time and turns into excellent fertiliser to spread on your garden and make your plants grow.

**energy** When you're talking about the environment, energy is the result of the burning of fossil fuels. Coal for example is a fossil fuel which is burned to make electricity, which is the energy that makes our lights, TVs, computers, etc, work. Petrol (made from a fossil fuel) is the chemical energy that makes your car go.

**Fair trade** If a product (food and drink, clothing, flowers) is labelled Fair trade, it means that whoever made the product, eg. banana farmers in Costa Rica, have been given a fair price. Find out more at fairtrade.org.uk.

**food miles** The distance food has to travel from the place where it's grown to the place where it's sold. The greater the number of food miles, the more energy is used and the greater the carbon footprint.
Green beans from Kenya = a lot of food miles.
Green beans from your local farmers' market = not many food miles.
Green beans from your garden = just a few food metres!

**fossil fuels** Fuels that are formed naturally in the Earth from animal or plant remains. Namely coal, oil and natural gas. If we keep using fossil fuels for our energy, eventually they will run out. Clean alternatives include wind power and solar (sun) power.

**global warming** The rise in the average temperature of the Earth as a result of the greenhouse effect. If we don't cut down on our $CO_2$ emissions, or aim to become carbon neutral, the Earth will keep getting warmer. A warmer world may mean crazy storms and floods, coastal towns being lost to the sea, and the extinction of some plants and animals.

**greenhouse effect** The rise in the Earth's temperature caused by certain gases in the atmosphere, including $CO_2$ and methane (one of the gases produced by landfill sites), trapping energy from the sun. Without the greenhouse effect we would live in an icy world because heat would escape back into space, but too much greenhouse effect is causing the Earth to heat up too much (see global warming).

**landfill** Huge places where our rubbish is dumped. Landfills are lined with clay and plastic and layered with soil. This blocks out light, moisture and oxygen, making it difficult for our trash to break down.

**offsetting** The term used to describe what we can do to cancel out our carbon footprint. Everything we do that releases $CO_2$ (watching TV, taking the bus, eating food with a lot of food miles, etc) we need to offset by doing something that helps the environment (recycling, growing our own food, planting a tree, etc).

**recycling** Put simply, this means using something again. Glass and plastic can be melted down and used again. Paper can be shredded, mulched and made into next week's Sunday papers. Old clothes can be customised and given a new lease of life. When it comes to recycling the mantra is, 'Once is not enough'.

**toxin** A poisonous substance produced naturally by living cells.

**UNESCO** The United Nations Educational, Scientific and Cultural Organization.

**volunteering** Offering your services for free to help a person, business, event or cause that you believe in.

# further information

### Animal Products
sustainweb.org

### Carbon Footprint
- carbonfootprint.com
- zerofootprintkids.com

### Careers
- peopleandplanet.org/ethicalcareers
- ethicalcareers.org

### Chocolate
- dubble.co.uk
- divinechocolate.com

### Climate Change & Global Warming
- news.bbc.co.uk/cbbcnews/hi/specials/ climate_change/default.stm
- justiceplus.org/Kids-Climate-Change- Links.htm

## Composting
- recyclenow.com
- vegweb.com/composting

## Cosmetics & Toiletries
greenyour.com/body/

## Eco Charities
- greenfinder.co.uk/companies/environmental-charities
- justgiving.com
- friendsoftheearth.co.uk
- greenpeace.co.uk
- wwf.org.uk (Worldwide Fund for Nature)

## Eco Shopping
- eattheseasons.co.uk
- ethiscore.org
- bbc.co.uk/food/food_matters
- sustainabletable.org
- theecologist.org
- fairtrade.org.uk
- charityshops.org.uk

## Greener Living
- bbc.co.uk/switch/surgery/advice/your_world/world/greener_living
- thedailygreen.com
- treehugger.com

## Growing your Own
- bbcgreen.com/food/grow-your-own/container-gardening
- backyardgardener.com/veg

## Landfill
weearth.com/go/voices/post/ 4209649

## Making your Voice Heard
Write to your MP/Councillor at writetothem.com

## Quizzes
biggreenswitch.co.uk/quizzes

## Recycling
- recyclenow.com
- recycling-guide.org.uk

## Volunteering
- do-it.org.uk
- volunteering.org.uk

## Water
waterwise.org.uk

# index